Thoughts From The Depths Of My Heart

Thoughts From The Depths Of My Heart

POEMS OF INSPIRATION AND COMFORT

Vanessa A. Sims

ISBN: 9780998903903
ISBN: 0998903906

www.vanessasims.com

Foreword

§

To be asked to write the foreword for a collection of beautifully composed sacred poetry --especially when asked by an author you love, admire, and respect -- is a request of high honor. On the pages that follow, you will discover the heart and soul of a gifted, Spirit-filled, and prolific writer. The artistic poetry of the writer is reminiscent of David playing the harp for the deeply troubled and distraught King Saul (I Samuel 16:23). As David's music eased the heart and mind of Saul; so, too, will the reader of these inspired writings find peace of mind, quietness of soul, and renewed strength.

Vanessa Sims is a courageous woman of abiding faith. While her writing reflects her keen cognitive abilities as a writer, she composes from her heart – even more so, she sings from her soul through rhyme, meter, and deep meaning using the written word as her medium.

It would be my own prayer that every person would have the opportunity to meet the poet who composed these life-transforming words – words born out of the very Word of God revealed in Jesus Christ. Even without meeting her personally, you will know her simply because her writing reflects who she is as beloved child of God, a faithful servant leader, and a true disciple of our Lord and Christ.

Anyone reading Mrs. Sims' work will be filled with every spiritual blessing from above – all throughout the year. It is a particularly helpful resource, however, for times such as Advent and Lent as we find ourselves filled joy and great expectancy for the coming of the Christ child and later journeying with Jesus through the wilderness for 40 days. The writer challenges us to explore forms of deeper relationship and closer communion with Jesus by offering helpful exercises of self-examination and critical analysis of our spiritual lives. In this artful and spiritual piece of work, you will find specific guiding questions to deepen your faith and broaden your spiritual horizons.

May you receive the same spiritual blessings in these inspirational writings that I have.

Rev. Dr. Jim Bowden – Lent, 2017, Pastor Trinity United Methodist Church

Acknowledgements

§

THIS COLLECTION OF SACRED POETRY is dedicated to my family, friends, and to those who need words of encouragement.

Thanks for allowing me to share these words with you.

Thanks to Dr. Tamara Lewis and Dr. Jeanne Stevenson-Moessner for their support and encouragement.

Thanks to my special friend Karen Shields-Smith for allowing me to use the beautiful photo on the front cover of this collection.

Thanks to my faith family at Trinity United Methodist Church, Denton, Texas who have encouraged me and allowed me to share my thoughts with them in sermons and during worship services.

Thanks to my mother Mary Emma Lyles for her love and for challenging me to complete this collection.

Special thanks to my husband Rev. Anthony Sims for his unwavering love and support.

Thank you Holy Spirit!

Introduction

§

FOR MANY YEARS I HAVE jotted down what I believed to be random thoughts. Words came to me in dreams, early in the morning hours, while waiting in line, during worship services, while driving, and during times of distress. During a season of distress, I found healing in writing down my thoughts. Of course, I thought that these were just my thoughts, thoughts to soothe only my soul. Lacking the confidence in writing, I dared not share these random thoughts with anyone.

My thoughts, not really! The Holy Spirit has a way of redirecting your thoughts and ownership of anything. After reading of an accidental death of a child, the Holy Spirit pricked me into action. I wrote words of comfort and sent them to the grandfather. Perhaps my thoughts could provide him and his family some measure of comfort. I was honored to have those words of comfort included in the funeral program.

In the spring of 2013, my mother was diagnosed with cancer, (stage IV). After hearing that doctor provide my mother with that awful news, my heart *ached*. After many sleepless nights and crying buckets of tears, I began to jot down my thoughts. Those thoughts resulted into the poem entitled *"Don't Fade Away Into the Sunset"* and the birthing of a Hope and Healing ministry. I shared those thoughts with the Life Matters Women's Cancer Support Group in Lawton, Oklahoma. Once again, people that were suffering encouraged me to continue writing and to publish my sacred poems.

One cold morning in January 2015, at Southern Methodist University, a mother shared the story of a fatal car accident that resulted in the death of her son. Listening to her story and seeing her pain, I shared my thoughts entitled *"I Just Slipped Away the Other Day"* with her. I was again honored to have the words of comfort shared with others during a memorial service. Although she was suffering, she *encouraged* me and helped usher in the confidence that I needed.

When I am faced with adversity and trials in my life, I seek comfort, strength, and protection in reading God's holy word. When doubt and fear haunt me, I pour out my soul to God. For me, self-examination and analysis of my spiritual life is important. I use biblical text for meditation, guidance, and self-examination. This method has enabled me to endure many trials and hardships therefore I have included self-examination worksheets in this collection.

This collection of sacred poetry is the result of the above and other similar experiences in my life. I pray that these words will inspire and bring comfort to many. I am thankful for the inspiration and the guidance of the Holy Spirit.

PRESENTED TO

_____

BY

_____

Table of Contents

For surely I know the plans I have for you, says the LORD,
plan for your welfare and not for harm,
to give you a future with hope.

JEREMIAH 29: 11

Words of Inspiration

You Are On A Journey to Greatness

§

It is no accident that you are here

So stop inhale, exhale, and release any thoughts of fears

You are on a journey to greatness

You were created unique, gifted, and destined to succeed

So push forth toward your destiny, God will provide all your needs

You are on a journey to greatness

God promises and grace has been extended to you

Your greatness also depends on what you choose to do

You are on a journey to greatness

Believe in the possibilities that you may not see

Trust that the Holy Spirit will lead you to where you need to be

You are on Journey to greatness

Embrace adversity and challenge that may come your way

Trust that your creator will always have the last say

You are on a Journey to Greatness

You Are On A Journey to Greatness

§

For the promise is for you, for your children, and for all who
are far away, everyone whom the Lord our God calls to him.

(ACTS 2: 39)

What are your spiritual goals?

1) _____

2) _____

3) _____

What are your personal goals?

1) _____

2) _____

3) _____

What are your career goals?

1) _____

2) _____

3) _____

"You Are A Gift From God"

§

You are a gift from God
Uniquely designed for a specific purpose

You are a gift from God
Created to be loved
Birthed to enjoy the creation of this great earth

You are a gift from God
God wrapped you up and delivered you

You are a gift from God
A gift unveiled, but it was no surprise

You are a gift from God
A precious gift, God shared with us

You are a gift from God
Let your heart respond to God's call

You are a gift from God
Tune out the negative voices and make the heavenly choices

You are a gift from God
We stand on the sidelines cheering for you

You are a gift from God
Reach forth into your destiny of greatness

You are a *gift* from God
We thank God for the beautiful gift of *you*!

You Are A Gift From God

*So God created humankind in his image, in the image of
God he created them: male and female he created them.*

(GENESIS 1:27)

Why did God Create You?

1) _____

2) _____

3) _____

What are your spiritual gifts?

1) _____

2) _____

3) _____

List three (3) positive thoughts about yourself.

1) _____

2) _____

3) _____

Greatness Is Waiting For You

§

Greatness is waiting for you

God has already made great plans for you

Greatness is waiting for you

If the pain of your past penetrate your thoughts

Know that greatness is waiting for you

Let your thoughts be focused on God's grace and love

Greatness is waiting for you

Listen only to God's spirit within you

Because greatness is waiting for you

Bring forth God's purpose for your life

Greatness is waiting for you

Unleash the gifts God embedded within you

Because greatness is waiting for you

Don't let invisible chains bind your greatness

Greatness is waiting for you

Step boldly into the grace of Greatness

Greatness is waiting for you

Because you were created by the almighty powerful God

Your Greatness Is Waiting for *YOU!*

Greatness Is Waiting For You

§

For surely I know the plans I have for you, says the LORD, plans
for your welfare and not for harm, to give you a future with hope.

JEREMIAH 29: 11

What is God's plan for your life?

1) _____

2) _____

3) _____

What are you doing to fulfill these plans?

1) _____

2) _____

3) _____

What is hindering you from accomplishing these plans?

1) _____

2) _____

3) _____

4) _____

I Am Wherever You Are

§

I created you and made you just like Me
I blessed you with everything from the land and the sea
I am wherever you are

I am there to greet you when you rise each new day
I am there because My words always has the final say
I am wherever you are

I am there when you experience sickness and pain
I want you to gain strength when you invoke My name
I am wherever you are

I am there when disappointments turn into fear
I am there because I promised that I would always be near
I am wherever you are

I am there catching you when you begin to fall
I am there because I can handle it all
I am wherever you are

I am there to forgive, cleanse, and to heal you
I am there because this is what I promised you that I would always do
I am wherever you are

I am there if you let My spirit guide you throughout the day
I am there to prepare you for that great judgment day
I am wherever you are
I am the one and only creator and faithful God

I Am Wherever You Are

§

Therefore prepare your minds for action; discipline
yourselves; set all your hope on the grace that Jesus
Christ will bring you when he is revealed.

(1 Peter 1: 13)

What does living by faith mean to you?

1) _____

2) _____

3) _____

What do you do when you are discouraged?

1) _____

2) _____

3) _____

How can you strengthen your faith?

1) _____

2) _____

3) _____

Just Trust Me

§

I am the God of your creation
I am the way to your salvation
Just Trust Me

I will restore you to Me
I will give you living water that will sustain you
Just Trust Me

I will guide and direct your life
I will light your lamp and lighten your path
Just Trust Me

I am your strength when you are weak
I am your refuge in time of troubles
Just Trust Me

I am not far from you
I am just a prayer away
Just Trust Me

I am the only one that can cleanse and heal you
I am the greatest physician
Just Trust Me

I will strengthen your broken heart
I will catch you when you begin to fall
Just Trust Me

I am your deliverance
I am limitless grace
Just Trust Me

I will keep My promises to you
I will keep you and bless you
JUST TRUST

Just Trust Me

§

Trust in the Lord with all your heart, and
do not rely on your own insight.

(PROVERBS 3: 5)

List three times when you totally trusted God.

1) _____

2) _____

3) _____

Why do you trust God to fulfill His promises?

1) _____

2) _____

3) _____

What does grace mean to you?

1) _____

2) _____

3) _____

When I

§

When I *rise* and greet each new day
I am confident that God's grace allowed me to stay

When I *listen* to what the Holy Spirit has to say
I am confident that I will enjoy this special day

When I *hear* the Holy Spirits' special voice
I am confident that I have no other choice

When I *plan* out this new day
I am glad that the Holy Spirit guides my way

When I *trust* that God's promises still stand for me
I am grateful for the blessings I allowed to

When I *give* thanks for the blessings of the day
I am so glad that God had the final say

When I *rejoice* and lay down at the end of the day
I know that it will be by God's grace if I greet another day

When I

§

From his fullness we have all received, grace upon grace.

(JOHN 1: 16)

How can you receive God's grace?

1) _____

2) _____

3) _____

List three times that you have received God's grace.

1) _____

2) _____

3) _____

List three times that you have shared God's grace.

1) _____

2) _____

3) _____

Don't Fade Away Into the Sunset

§

God uniquely designed you

Who you are makes a difference

Don't just fade away into the sunset

There's a light burning bright inside of you

Re-kindle the light that burned so brightly within you

Don't just fade away into the sunset

Share the light that God gave you

Your shining light is needed to guide those who are in darkness

Don't just fade away into the sunset

Who you are makes a difference

Your compassion, kindness, and generosity is needed

Don't just fade away into the sunset

You have so much love to share

You are a great blessing

Don't just fade away into the sunset

Don't Fade Away Into the Sunset

§

Let us lay aside every weight and the sin that clings so closely,
and let us run with perseverance the race that is set before
us, looking to Jesus the pioneer and perfecter of our faith.

(HEBREWS 12: 1)

List some trials that you have endured.

1) _____

2) _____

3) _____

List three people that you share your struggles with.

1) _____

2) _____

List three scriptures that help you endure trials or suffering in your life.

1) _____

2) _____

3) _____

I Am The God

§

I am the God that created you
I am the God that breathed life into you and blessed you
I am that God that provides steadfast love
I am the God that provides you hope
I am The God

I am the God that provides you strength when you are weak
I am the God that's with you in the time of trouble
I am the God that will lift you up when you fall down
I am the God that will not forsake you
I Am The God

I am the God that brings you peace
I am the God that can strengthen your heart
I am the God that can sustain and heal you
I am the God that answers your prayers
I Am The God

I am the God of grace and mercy
I am the God that is always faithful
I am the God of refuge
I am the God of your salvation
I Am The God

I Am Who I Am

Inspired by the Book of Psalms

I Am The God

§

For he will command his angels concerning
you to guard you in all your ways.

(Psalms 91: 11)

What is preventing you from trusting in God's promises?

1) _____

2) _____

3) _____

List three scriptures that relate to trusting God.

1) _____

2) _____

3) _____

How can you strengthen your trust in God?

1) _____

2) _____

3) _____

Come to me, all you that are weary and are carrying
heavy burdens, and I will give you rest.

(MATTHEW 11: 28)

Words Of Comfort

I went to Heaven the other Day

I went to heaven the other day
I told God, I was tired of my earthly stay
Both of you were special to me in many ways
Please know that I loved you every day

I went to heaven the other day
God listened to what I had to say
I was tired of the heartaches, the sickness, and the pain
I simply requested God to call my name

It probably seems like only yesterday
When we shared our love in the most beautiful ways
Cherish those memories and celebrate our years
Don't live your life in misery with constant tears

I quietly went to heaven the other day
Because I saw God's hand reaching out to greet me
Oh this beautiful heaven, I wish you could see
Know that heaven is a holy place and a great place to be

Keep your faith in God and love each other
Remember these parting words from your mother
God will also listen to what you have to say

I slipped away and went to my heavenly home the other day
Because God knew I had already completed my earthly stay
Please know this is where I longed to be
I sure hope that this beautiful heaven you will also be able to see

Love You, Mom

Dedicated to Tony Hall and Russell Hall

I Am There

§

I am there when you begin each day
Ready to hug you in a very special way

I am there when your mind wonders to the memories of our past,
Hope that you remember the loving words we shared last

I am there hoping to see your beautiful smile
I was so glad that it was gone for only a little while

I am up there looking down at you from up above
Thank God He gave me a mother filled with so much love

I am there on all your special days
Ready to listen to what you have to say

If you are sadden by the thoughts that I am forever gone
Look up, I am not far away, I am in God's heavenly home

I am there thanking God for a beautiful mother like you
Your love was immeasurable and I hope you knew I love you dearly too

My spirit will always be there with you!

Written for Dr. Jeanne Stevenson-Moessner

My Body is Gone But You Are Not Alone

You may not be able to hear me, see me, or touch me
But know that I am where God wants me to be
If you need me, just simply call my name
And just look at me in the nearest picture frame
My Body is Gone, But You will never be alone

Remember my touch and remember my smile
Know that we will be separated from a little while
It was my time to go to my heavenly home, only God knows the reasons
God shared me with you to enjoy for only limited seasons
My Body is Gone, But You will never be alone

If you feel you need to cry
Find peace in God's love, know that He loves you and so did I
Know that my spirit will always be near
So please don't live your life with constant tears
My Body is Gone, But You will never be alone

When you need comfort because of lingering pain
All you need to do is call out my name
I'll surround you with my spirit
Be still so that you may feel it
My Body is Gone, But you will never be alone

Although I'm gone to my heavenly home
Know that I love you dearly and you will never be alone

Know That God

§

Your pain might seem so fresh and unbearable today
Know that God is always ready to listen to what you have to say

You may be unsure what will happen tomorrow
Know that God will help you through all of your sorrows

It may seem that trials keep coming your way
Know that God's power can help you make it through each day

You may think you growing weaker each and every day
Know that God is able to strengthen you totally in every way

It may seems no one truly understands
Know that God can heal any heartache; just release your cares into His
hands

It may seem at times that you are all alone
Know that God is with you when everyone else is gone

You might not know how to continue running this life's race
Know that God has extended to you unlimited grace

You may question whether God is looking out for you from up above
Know that God is always ready to wrap you in His love

God is looking forward to seeing you too in His heavenly place
But until then, *Know that God* wants you to enjoy his unwavering
love and grace

For surely I know the plans I have for you, says the LORD,
plans for your welfare and not for harm,
to give you a future with hope.

JEREMIAH 29: 11

ABOUT THE AUTHOR

§

VANESSA A. SIMS HAS BEEN in servant ministry for over 35 years. She is the founder of Thou Art My Sister LLC. She also founded, "The Little Sister Mentoring Program", a ministry founded to uplift and to inspire female youth and young adults.

Serving alongside her husband, Rev. Anthony Sims, in pastoral ministry for over 25 years provided her teaching, preaching, and evangelistic opportunities. She quickly learned that by allowing the Holy Spirit to lead and guide her that she could share the good news of God's unlimited amazing grace, love, and power.

Vanessa inspires others by sharing her unique story of God's amazing grace and unwavering love. During her faith journey, Vanessa earned a Master of Theological Studies from Southern Methodist University - Perkins

School of Theology, Dallas, Texas and a Certificate of Theological Studies from Texas Christian University - Brite Divinity School, Fort Worth, Texas. Vanessa credits her study of *"Practical Theology"* at the University of Cambridge, Wesley House, Cambridge, England, for her simple and practical approach to ministry.

Thoughts From The Depths of My Heart

Vanessa A. Sims

www.vanessasims.com

Greatness Is Waiting For You!